HOLY ROAR

SEVEN WORDS THAT WILL CHANGE THE WAY YOU WORSHIP

STUDY GUIDE | 4 SESSIONS

CHRIS TOMLIN *and* DARREN WHITEHEAD
with BETH GRAYBILL

THOMAS NELSON
Since 1798

Holy Roar Study Guide

© 2019 by Chris Tomlin and Darren Whitehead

Published in Nashville, Tennessee, by Thomas Nelson. Thomas Nelson is a registered trademark of HarperCollins Christian Publishing, Inc.

Published in association with Anvil II Management, Inc.

All Scripture quotations, unless otherwise indicated, are taken from The Holy Bible, New International Version®, NIV®. Copyright © 1973, 1978, 1984, 2011 by Biblica, Inc.™ Used by permission. All rights reserved worldwide.

Scripture quotations marked ESV are taken from The Holy Bible, English Standard Version. 2016. Copyright © 2001 by Crossway, a publishing ministry of Good News Publishers. The ESV® text has been reproduced in cooperation with and by permission of Good News Publishers. Unauthorized reproduction of this publication is prohibited. All rights reserved.

Scripture quotations marked NKJV are taken from the New King James Version®. Copyright © 1982 by Thomas Nelson. Used by permission. All rights reserved.

"How Great Is Our God" by Chris Tomlin, Jesse Reeves, and Ed Cash. Copyright © 2004 worshiptogether.com Songs/sixsteps Music/ASCAP (adm. @ CapitolCMGPublishing. com)/ Alletrop Music/BMI All rights reserved. Used by permission.

"Holy Is the Lord" by Chris Tomlin and Louie Giglio. Copyright © 2003 worshiptogether.com Songs (ASCAP) sixsteps Music (ASCAP) Vamos Publishing (ASCAP) (adm. at CapitolCMGPublishing.com) All rights reserved. Used by permission.

"Good Good Father" by Pat Barrett and Anthony Brown. Copyright © 2014 Housefires Sounds (ASCAP) Tony Brown Publishing Designee (NS) Common Hymnal Digital (BMI) worshiptogether.com Songs (ASCAP) sixsteps Music (ASCAP) Vamos Publishing (ASCAP) Capitol CMG Paragon (BMI) (adm. at CapitolCMGPublishing.com) All rights reserved. Used by permission.

"I Lift My Hands" by Chris Tomlin, Louie Giglio, and Matt Maher. Copyright © 2014 Housefires Sounds (ASCAP) Tony Brown Publishing Designee (NS) Common Hymnal Digital (BMI) worshiptogether.com Songs (ASCAP) sixsteps Music (ASCAP) Vamos Publishing (ASCAP) Capitol CMG Paragon (BMI) (adm. at CapitolCMGPublishing. com) All rights reserved. Used by permission.

Thomas Nelson titles may be purchased in bulk for educational, business, fundraising, or sales promotional use. For information, please e-mail SpecialMarkets@ThomasNelson. com.

ISBN 978-0-310-09871-3

First Printing December 2018 / Printed in the United States of America

CONTENTS

INTRODUCTION

A few years ago, a woman went on vacation with her family to a well-known theme park. One evening, they all decided to take a break from the heat and long lines and watch a stage version of the infamous movie-turned-musical *The Lion King*. Like everyone else around them, the family was enamored with the costumes and props, as well as the singing, acting, and dancing.

Near the end of the musical, when the new Lion King appeared on stage in celebration, the sold-out audience erupted in applause. Everyone stood to their feet, hands raised, dancing and singing along with the cast of characters in celebration of this beautiful story. At that moment, with her arms raised high, the woman heard a faint whisper: *"So you can raise your hands for the Lion King, but you can't raise your hands for the King of Kings?"*

As the crowd continued to cheer, the woman sat back down in her seat. You see, she had grown up in a well-meaning church, where the preference during worship was for the people in the pews to hold on to their hymnals instead of raising their hands in celebration. *"Lift your voice, not your hands"* was the subtle message the woman had heard and seen modelled by her fellow church-goers. Any sort of praise celebration was meant to be *personal* and *internal* . . . anything else was just too distracting to her fellow worshippers.

Perhaps you can relate. If you have spent your early years influenced by this mentality of praise, it can lead to you feeling uncomfortable with outward displays of emotion and enthusiasm. And, certainly, there are times when you *should* be silent, listening and reflecting on a message and expressing your praise in a quiet manner. As the apostle Paul instructed his churches, "Everything should be done in a fitting and orderly way" (1 Corinthians 14:40).

But when we explore the Bible—and especially the worship practices in the Old Testament—we also find people offering enthusiastic praises of passion to God. This should lead us to conclude there *are* times when God wants us to outwardly express the celebration we feel in our hearts as we consider his greatness and express our praise to him. As King Solomon wrote, "There is a time for everything . . . a time to weep *and a time to laugh,* a time to mourn *and a time to dance*" (Ecclesiastes 3:1,4, emphasis added).

In the book of Psalms, there are seven primary Hebrew words translated into English as *praise.* Each of these words—*halal, shabach, yadah, barak, tehillah, zamar,* and *towdah*—have distinct, important, and praise-altering implications. This study is an attempt to share the depth of meaning found in those seven words as we explore them together.

We pray this study, and the accompanying book of the same name, become a resource to help you better understand just what it means when the Bible says, "Praise the Lord!" We hope it changes the way you worship and gives you "permission" to join in the practices of the praise. We pray it urges you to join in and become a part of the *holy roar* of God's people.

Are you ready? Let's jump in.

HOW TO USE THIS GUIDE

The *Holy Roar* video study is designed to be experienced in a group setting such as a Bible study, Sunday school class, or any small group gathering. Our hope is that you walk away from this study feeling complete freedom to express your praise to God—regardless of your background, church setting, or personality preferences.

Each session of this study begins with a brief welcome section and opening questions to get you thinking about the topic. You will then watch a video message with Darren Whitehead and Chris Tomlin and engage in some directed small-group discussion. You will close each session with a time of reflection, response, and worship as a group.

During the week, maximize the impact of the study by engaging in the between-sessions personal studies that have been provided. Treat each personal study section like a devotional and use them in whatever way works best for your schedule. Note that these are not required, but they will be beneficial to you. Beginning in session two, you will also be given the opportunity to share any thoughts, questions, or takeaways you have from your personal study.

Each person in the group should have his or her own copy of this study guide. You are also encouraged to have a copy of the *Holy Roar* book, as reading the book alongside the curriculum will provide you with deeper insights and make the journey more meaningful. See the "For Next Week" section at the end of each between-sessions section for the chapters in the book that correspond to material you and your group will be discussing.

Keep in mind the video teachings, discussion questions, and activities are simply meant to help you engage with the material you will be covering each week. As you go through this study, be open for what God is saying to you and how you feel He is leading you to apply what you are discovering. As you do this, your life will become a living expression of praise to God.

———————————

Note: If you are a group leader, there are additional resources provided in the back of this guide to help you lead your group members through the study.

one

THE SHOUT OF PRAISE

The most valuable thing the psalms do for me is to express the same delight in God which made David dance.... [They] stand out as something astonishingly robust, virile, and spontaneous; something we may regard with an innocent envy and may hope to be infected by as we read.

C.S. Lewis, *Reflections on the Psalms*

הָלַל

HALAL

haw-lal': To boast. To rave. To shine.
To celebrate. To be clamorously foolish.

Let them praise [halal] *his name with dancing
and make music to him with timbrel and harp.*

Psalm 149:3

שָׁבַח

SHABACH

shaw-bakh' : To address in a loud tone.
To shout. To commend, glory, and triumph.

One generation shall praise [shabach]
*Your works to another, and shall
declare Your mighty acts.*

Psalm 145:4 NKJV

WELCOME

Picture this—you're standing in the middle of five million people the moment the Chicago Cubs win the World Series. For the past century, dedicated fans have been saying hopeful prayers for their team as they watched them play at Wrigley Field, or listened to their games on the radio, or watched on their television sets as they gathered around the dinner table. But all seemingly to no avail . . . until the Cubs make this eleventh appearance in the World Series in 2016. Finally, after *108* long, long, long years of waiting, the Cubs have claimed the pennant!

Whether you're a baseball fan or not, you can imagine what it would be like to stand in the middle of that crowd, with people yelling, cheering, and even crying tears of joy. Hands are lifted. Towels and T-shirts are waved high in the air. People share hugs and high-fives and give shouts of joy—all in the name of celebration. Perhaps you've experienced something similar during a raucous concert, a sporting event, or some kind of gathering. No matter where you've experienced it, you know that when you're in the middle of *that* kind of celebration, you can't help but feel the excitement and energy pulse through your veins.

Or maybe you've experienced this type of celebration at a wedding. You know the one . . . that reception where it seemed the entire guest list was out there on the dance floor. Maybe your preference was to stay on the edge of the dance floor, where you felt a bit more comfortable—gently swaying back and forth to the beat. Or maybe you were the one out there, with all eyes on you (and your dance moves) at center stage. Either way, there was just something about this collective celebration of movement that just drew you in. There was something that made you want to celebrate with *others* and have crazy fun *together*.

When you experience moments like this, it's easy to see that the God of the universe made each of us to praise him with abandon, like foolish but fun-loving children, together in unity. God wants our full and free expression of praise—and his desire for our praise isn't contingent on our personalities, our feelings, or our comfort zones. In fact, God doesn't just *desire* our worship but also *requires* our worship. And as we see in the book of Psalms and other places in the Bible, that worship often takes the form of exuberant shouts of praise!

SHARE

Welcome to the first session of *Holy Roar.* If you or any of your fellow group members do not know one another, take a few minutes to introduce yourselves. Then, to get things started, discuss one of the following questions:

- Have you ever been to an event where there was a lot of loud celebration—a concert, a sporting event, a musical or show? If so, what was it like?

—*or*—

- What does the phrase "shout of praise" mean to your church family? How is it expressed in your weekly worship?

WATCH

Play the video segment for session one. As you watch, use the following outline to record any thoughts or concepts that stand out to you.

Notes

There are seven Hebrew words translated as *praise* in the book of Psalms . . .

The Hebrew word *halal* means _____
_____. It is where we get the word
_____.

> *Let them praise* [halal] *his name with*
> *dancing and make music to him with*
> *timbrel and harp* (Psalm 149:3).

> *Let everything that has breath praise*
> [halal] *the LORD!* (Psalm 150:6).

The essence of *halal* is . . .

Another aspect of the word *halal* is . . .

I will celebrate [halal] *before the* LORD. *I will*
become even more undignified than this . . .
(2 Samuel 6:21–22).

The Hebrew word *shabach* means _____
_____. It involves the idea of God's people
coming together to . . .

One generation shall commend [shabach]
your works to another (Psalm 145:4 ESV).

Every time the body of Christ gathers together, what they are
celebrating is . . .

How Great is Our God—why this is an anthem of praise . . .

*L*ORD *my God, you are very great; you are clothed with splendor and majesty. The L*ORD *wraps himself in light as with a garment; he stretches out the heavens like a tent and lays the beams of his upper chambers on their waters* (Psalm 104:1–3).

"You're the name above all names"—*shabach* happens when people . . .

DISCUSS

Take a few minutes with your group members to discuss what you just watched and explore these concepts in Scripture.

1. What are a few key points that stood out to you from this session?

2. Think about the stories Darren told of the Jewish wedding and the Chicago Cubs winning the World Series after a 108-year drought. What are some other ways people celebrate *halal* and *shabach* as a culture outside of church?

3. Read aloud Psalm 104. What are some reasons King David lists in these verses for praising the Lord? Which of these stand out to you?

4. How do David's words remind you of all God has done? Why is it often easy to overlook these "simple" things God does all the time? Why is it important to remember these?

5. Read aloud Psalm 150. How is God celebrated in this passage? What does it look like for "everything that has breath" to "praise the Lord"?

6. How does your church celebrate *halal* and *shabach*? In what ways is this the same or different as the way you see it celebrated in these psalms?

RESPOND

Close out today's session by briefly reviewing the outline for the video teaching and any notes you took. In the space below, write down the most significant point you took away from the session and why it is meaningful for you. If there's time, share your answer with the group.

WORSHIP

Consider worshiping together as you close out your group discussion. Play "How Great Is Our God" on your streaming device, or ask someone in your group if they would be willing to play it on a musical instrument. Focus on the words of the song and think about the ways in which they capture the essence of *halal* and *shabach*. Close by spending a few minutes in prayer together.

How Great Is Our God

The splendor of a King, clothed in majesty
Let all the Earth rejoice
All the Earth rejoice

He wraps himself in light
And darkness tries to hide
And trembles at His voice
Trembles at His voice

How great is our God, sing with me
How great is our God, and all will see
How great, how great is our God

Age to age He stands
And time is in His hands
Beginning and the end

The Godhead Three in One
Father Spirit Son
The Lion and the Lamb
The Lion and the Lamb

How great is our God, sing with me
How great is our God, and all will see
How great, how great is our God

Name above all names
Worthy of our praise
My heart will sing
How great is our God

You're the name above all names
You are worthy of our praise
And my heart will sing
How great is our God

How great is our God, sing with me
How great is our God, and all will see
How great, how great is our God

How great is our God, sing with me
How great is our God, and all will see
How great, how great is our God

The whole world sings, the whole world sings
How great is our God
How great is our God
How great, how great is our God

Songwriters: Chris Tomlin, Jesse Reeves, and Ed Cash.
From the album *Arriving*.

one

BETWEEN-SESSIONS
PERSONAL STUDY

Reflect on the content you've covered this week in *Holy Roar* by engaging in any or all of the following between-sessions activities. The time you invest will be well spent, so let God use it to draw you closer to him. At your next meeting, share with your group any key points or insights that stood out to you as you spent this time with the Lord.

DAY ONE: *HALAL* THROUGH THE EYES OF THE ISRAELITES

Seek

■ Read Leviticus chapters 23 and 25. The author of these passages in the Old Testament uses the word *halal* to describe the way people might celebrate a festival. What kind of festivals does the Lord direct his people to celebrate throughout these two chapters?

■ Which one stands out the most to you? Why?

■ What can we learn from the ancient Israelites regarding the way they celebrated special moments and seasons during their time?

■ What are the special moments in your life that are cause for celebration?

■ What are the special moments in your church community that are cause for celebration?

Reflect

■ Think about the story Chris told of writing the song "How Great Is Our God" and his experience with the Watoto Children's Choir from Uganda. Is there praise you long to give to God today? In what ways has God been a "great God" in your life?

■ Is there a particular song or anthem that speaks to you as you offer your praise to God? Write down a few words of the song that come to mind.

Take time to pray today. Ask God to open your eyes, your heart, and your mind to the opportunities for celebration around you. And as you celebrate those special moments and special people, may you also offer a praise of celebration to God for his goodness in your life.

Apply

Pick a special occasion or moment to celebrate today. Is there a season when God provided for you or came through in ways only he can do? Just like the journey of the Israelites, there are many moments to celebrate if you're willing to pause and reflect back over God's goodness in your life. Write a note of praise, make a special meal, create something that reminds you of that time, sing, or dance in celebration. Celebrate in whatever way seems most natural to you.

DAY TWO: *HALAL* THROUGH THE EYES OF KING DAVID

Seek

■ Read Psalm 22:22–26, Psalm 69:30–36, and Psalm 109:30–31. These verses were written by King David in first person but were often sung corporately in ancient Israel. What stands out to you in each of these psalms? Why?

■ Imagine a gathering where people are singing your words of prayer and praise to God. What specific prayers or praises would they be singing?

■ Consider your community. What specific prayers or praises would you want to sing on behalf of your friends, family, co-workers, students, neighbors, and others?

■ How would you describe your preferred style of prayer and praise?

■ How would others describe your preferred style of prayer and praise? If there's a difference between your answers for these two questions, why do you think this is the case?

Reflect

■ During the teaching this week, Chris mentioned how the song "How Great Is Our God" for him has become an anthem of prayer and praise. What are some songs that you would consider an "anthem of corporate praise"? Why do those songs resonate with you?

■ What is the power of simply declaring the greatness of God? When are some times in your life when you found that this was your prayer?

Take time to pray today. Ask God to remind you of moments when you have been impacted by corporate prayer and praise. Sit for a few moments with those memories. Consider what you were thinking, feeling, and experiencing in those moments. Thank God for the gift of those corporate worship experiences and praise God for his presence in your life.

Apply

If you could pray or praise on behalf of someone close to you, what would you say or sing? Write down your prayer or praise on behalf of that person and share it with them in a text, email, or a personal note. Also reach out to a close friend or trusted family member to share a specific prayer or praise for your own life. Ask them to pray with you and for you.

DAY THREE: *HALAL* AND *SHABACH* IN THE NEW TESTAMENT

Seek

■ There are many passages in the Old Testament that speak of praising God and celebrating his festivals, but there are also numerous stories of praising God in the New Testament. Read Luke 15:11–32 and Acts 3:1–10. What stands out to you in these two stories?

■ What did praise and celebration look like in the story of the Lost Son?

■ What would you be feeling or thinking if you returned home after running away and received this kind of celebration?

■ What did praise and celebration look like in the story of the lame beggar healed in the temple?

■ What would you be feeling or thinking if you were healed after a lifetime of not being able to walk?

■ When there are good things to celebrate in your own life, how do you stay mindful of honoring God with your praise and worship?

■ Is there a recent celebration in your life where you neglected to give God praise? If so, name it and take a moment to offer words or songs of praise to God right now.

Reflect

■ During the teaching this week, Chris mentioned there are moments for everything—for kneeling, being quiet, lifting your hands . . . and moments "where it's just a full shout out to God in celebration to God." How do you react to the idea of this type of worship? When was the last time (if ever) that you expressed a "holy roar" to God in praise?

■ Think about situations where people feel the freedom to be *loud* and *clamorously foolish* (such as a sporting event, a concert, or some other type of public celebration). What are the marks of that kind of celebration? What is it about the environment that makes it comfortable to celebrate in those ways?

Take time to pray today. Ask God to give you more freedom in the way you praise and celebrate. Ask him to show you what moves you to want to yell and cheer. Thank God for those moments of unsubdued praise and commit to worshiping him in the same way.

Apply

The next time you are at a concert, a sporting event, or are enjoying a rowdy game where you lift your voice and your hands in celebration, stop and consider celebrating God in that moment as well. As you become mindful of giving "thanks in all circumstances" (1 Thessalonians 5:18), you will carry the holy expressions of *halal* and *shabach* with you everywhere you go.

DAY FOUR: *SHABACH* IN THE WILDERNESS

Seek

■ Read Psalm 63. David penned this song when he was a fugitive from the jealous King Saul and was hiding in the wilderness. What stands out to you in this passage?

■ Imagine that you are in David's situation. You have been anointed as the next king of Israel (see 1 Samuel 16:1–13) but are now running for your life and hiding out in caves. What would you be tempted to think about God given these circumstances? What did David think about God?

■ Have you ever had your own "desert wilderness" season? How hard or easy was it for you to praise God in the middle of that season?

■ If you are in the middle of that season right now, what praise do you need to cry out to God? What questions do you have for God? Remember that God is big enough to handle *all* of your disappointment, anger, frustration, *and* praise at the same time.

Reflect

■ Listen to or read through the lyrics of the song "How Great Is Our God" with your "desert wilderness" season in mind. What is it like for you to experience the words of this song with that difficult season in mind? What thoughts, questions or images are stirring for you?

■ What words or phrases in this song stand out to you in a new way?

Take time to pray today. Ask God to give you freedom in the way you praise and celebrate. Ask him to show you what moves you to want to yell and cheer and be wild and crazy. Thank God for those moments of unsubdued praise and commit to worshiping him in the same way.

Apply

Pick an anthem of praise you can sing for a wilderness season you are facing. What song best describes your challenges or inspires you toward hope and praise? If this exercise brings comfort or healing to your soul, go back to past wilderness seasons and consider which anthem would have described that particular time in your life.

DAY FIVE: A HOLY ROAR

Seek

■ Read Psalm 104 and 145. Consider all of the reasons listed in these two psalms to give *shabach* praise to God. Which reasons stand out to you? Pick a few and write them down here.

■ In Psalm 104:34, the author writes, "May my meditation be pleasing to [God], as I rejoice in the Lord." What does your "meditation" look like? (*Praying, singing, reading, silence, solitude?*) Why do you think this is pleasing to God?

■ In Psalm 145:4, the author writes, "One generation commends your works to another; they tell of your mighty acts." How have you been told of God's works and mighty acts by the older generations around you?

■ How are you telling the younger generation about God's works and mighty acts? Considering the way our culture has changed over the years, how is the way you're telling the younger generation about God different than the way you were told?

Reflect

■ Select a few verses from Psalm 104 or 145 that speak about the greatness of God. What is one situation you are currently facing that you will commit to trusting completely to him?

■ How does reflecting on these passages that speak of God's greatness help you to believe that he is willing and able to handle those situations?

Take time to pray today. Ask God to give you new perspective on ways to express *halal* and *shabach* even when life is difficult. Thank God for creating you with an innate desire to praise, to cheer, and to be loud and joyful in celebration.

Apply

Put *halal* and *shabach* into action this week. Perhaps you don't feel comfortable doing this for the first time at church . . . but that doesn't mean you can't worship this way in your car (remember Darren's car story?), or in your dorm room, or in your living room, or in your office, or in the great outdoors. It's okay if you need to practice these expressions of praise in private so that you feel the freedom to praise and celebrate in public!

FOR NEXT WEEK

Use the space below to write down any key points or questions that you want to bring to the next group meeting. Review the content from chapters 2 and 7 in *Holy Roar* that were covered this week, and for the next session, read chapters 1 and 5.

two

THE POSTURE OF PRAISE

The inward attitude certainly holds first place in prayer, but outward signs, kneeling, uncovering the head, lifting up the hands, have a twofold use. The first is that we may employ all our members for the glory and worship of God; secondly, that we are, so to speak, jolted out of our laziness by this help. There is also a third use in solemn and public prayer, because in this way the sons of God profess their piety, and they inflame each other with reverence of God.

John Calvin,
Commentary on Acts

יָדָה

YADAH

yaw-daw' : To revere or worship
with extended hands. To hold out the
hands. To throw a stone or arrow.

May the peoples praise [yadah] *you, God;*
may all the peoples praise [yadah] *you.*

Psalm 67:3

בָּרַךְ

BARAK

baw-rak' : To kneel. To bless God (as an act
of adoration). To praise. To salute. To thank.

Enter his gates with thanksgiving and
his courts with praise; give thanks to
him and praise [barak] *his name.*

Psalm 100:4

WELCOME

A few years ago, a man decided to run the Philadelphia Half Marathon. Less than one month earlier, the Philadelphia Phillies had won the World Series (yes, another World Series mention, but stay with us), so it seemed like a good idea to wear a Phillies jersey for the race. As the man rounded the homestretch of the 13.1-mile race in front of the Philadelphia Art Museum steps, he heard the crowd start to cheer loudly.

The man assumed the cheering was because of the Phillies jersey he was wearing. So he picked up speed and raised his arms high in celebration as he ran the last 100 yards of the race. It was only when he crossed the finish line—arms still raised—that he realized the crowd was cheering because the winner of the *full* marathon had crossed the finish line at the same time. The winner of that race, who the man saw down on his knees in celebration, had run *26.2* miles in the same time it had taken him to run 13.1 miles!

Have you ever noticed the way athletes respond when they score a goal, cross the finish line, or win a game? Many of them raise their hands or fall down on their knees in celebration. What stands out about this man's story is that the cheering of the crowd inspired him to raise his arms high in celebration. The winner of the full marathon, however, fell to his knees in celebration (and probably exhaustion too).

In the book of Psalms, we find two Hebrew words for *praise* that capture these different postures of worship. *Yadah* represents the outward expression—the celebration with your arms raised high. *Barak* represents the more introspective expression—the act of praising God down on your knees. Both of these responses are postures of praise to God!

So here's the deal . . . no one can determine the way you give God your praise. Only you. So don't let someone else's opinions keep you from praising God. And don't hold back your praise just because lifting your hands or kneeling is out of your comfort zone. You can express the love and admiration you feel toward God on the inside with an outside posture of praise.

SHARE

Welcome to the second session of *Holy Roar*. If you or any of your fellow group members do not know one another, take a few minutes to introduce yourselves and share any insights you wrote down from last week's personal study. Then, to kick things off for the group time, discuss one of the following questions:

- Do you have a story similar to the one you just read that you would be willing to share with the group—a story where you thought the cheering from others was because of you when really it wasn't?

—or—

- Do you remember the first time you lifted your hands in celebration during worship? What was that experience like for you?

WATCH

Play the video segment for session two. As you watch, use the following outline to record any thoughts or concepts that stand out to you.

Notes

Being invited to the "other" kind of church . . .

The Hebrew word *yadah* means _____
_____. In the Old Testament, it is used
a couple of times to refer to _____
or _____.

> *May the peoples praise* [yadah] *you, God; may*
> *all the peoples praise* [yadah] *you* (Psalm 67:3).

When your desire to express your love to Jesus surpasses your
self-consciousness . . .

God's call is that we be people who follow his command to . . .

The Hebrew word *barak* means _____
_____. In the ancient world, it involved the
idea of _____ before the king and keeping _____ contact
with him or keeping your _____ fixed on him. *Barak* is the
posture of . . .

> *Enter his gates with thanksgiving* [yadah] *and his courts with praise; give thanks to him and praise* [barak] *his name* (Psalm 100:4).

When we kneel before God, it is as if we are saying to him . . .

> *Holy, holy, holy is the* LORD *Almighty; the whole earth is full of his glory* (Isaiah 6:3).

What Isaiah saw in his vision . . .

Holy Is the Lord—a song of heaven . . .

DISCUSS

Take a few minutes with your group members to discuss what you just watched and explore these concepts in Scripture.

1. What are a few key points that stood out to you from this session?

2. Consider Darren's story about visiting "another" kind of church and Chris's story about the woman in his church who was raising her hands in worship. How can you relate to either of these stories? What tends to be your posture when you worship God?

3. How does your personality influence the style of praise you find most comfortable? Have you ever been in a situation where you were uncomfortable with the outward signs of expression or praise? Explain.

4. Read aloud Psalm 67 and 134. What are some of the reasons the psalmist gives as to why the people of God praise him? How are they instructed to praise him?

5. Read aloud Psalm 44:1-8. What are some reasons you have been told to praise God—by your family, your friends, or your church? What reasons do you share with others to encourage them to praise God?

6. How does your church celebrate *yadah* and *barak*? Is one more acceptable than the other in your church community? If so, why do you think that is the case?

RESPOND

Close out today's session by briefly reviewing the outline for the video teaching and any notes you took. In the space below, write down the most significant point you took away from the session and why it is meaningful for you. If there's time, share your answer with the group.

WORSHIP

Consider worshiping together as you close out your group discussion. Play "Holy Is the Lord" on your streaming device, or ask someone in your group if they would be willing to play this song on a musical instrument. Focus on the words of the song and think about the ways in which they capture the essence of *yadah* and *barak*. Close by spending a few minutes in prayer together.

Holy Is the Lord

We stand and lift up our hands
For the joy of the Lord is our strength
We bow down and worship Him now
How great, how awesome is He

And together we sing

Holy is the Lord God Almighty
The earth is filled with His glory
Holy is the Lord God Almighty
The earth is filled with His glory
The earth is filled with His glory

We stand and lift up our hands
For the joy of the Lord is our strength
We bow down and worship Him now
How great, how awesome is He

And together we sing
Everyone sing

Holy is the Lord God Almighty
The earth is filled with His glory
Holy is the Lord God Almighty
The earth is filled with His glory
The earth is filled with His glory

It's rising up all around
It's the anthem of the Lord's renown

It's rising up all around
It's the anthem of the Lord's renown

And together we sing
Everyone sing

Holy is the Lord God Almighty
The earth is filled with His glory
Holy is the Lord God Almighty
The earth is filled with His glory
The earth is filled with His glory

The earth is filled with His glory

Holy, holy is the Lord Almighty, holy, holy
Holy, holy is the Lord Almighty, holy, holy
Holy, holy is the Lord Almighty, holy, holy

Songwriters: Chris Tomlin and Louie Giglio.
From the album *Arriving*.

two

BETWEEN-SESSIONS PERSONAL STUDY

Reflect on the content you've covered this week in *Holy Roar* by engaging in any or all of the following between-sessions activities. The time you invest will be well spent, so let God use it to draw you closer to him. At your next meeting, share with your group any key points or insights that stood out to you as you spent this time with the Lord.

DAY ONE: *YADAH* THROUGH THE EYES OF THE ISRAELITES

Seek

■ Read Jeremiah 50:4–20 and Lamentations 3:49–60. The author of these passages in the Old Testament uses the word *yadah* to describe shooting an arrow from a bow or extending one's arms to throw rocks. What does this say about the worshipper's posture when it comes to expressing *yadah* praise to God?

■ Which of these two images—shooting arrows and extending your arms—stands out to you the most when you picture yadah praise? Why?

■ Raising one's hands is a sign of surrender. Just think about what law enforcement officials say when they catch a person suspected of a crime: "Put your hands in the air!" In what ways do you experience this kind of vulnerability to God when you lift your hands in worship?

■ What are you essentially saying to God when you extend your hands in praise? What are some things in your life that you still need to surrender to him?

Reflect

■ Think about the story Chris shared about writing the song "Holy Is the Lord." The words for this song were inspired by the apostle John's vision of heaven in Revelation 4:8, as it was foretold in Isaiah 6:3. How do you envision the praise of heaven?

■ Is there another song or anthem that makes you think about what the praise of heaven must be like? Why that particular song?

Take time to pray today. Ask God to give you freedom in worship. Consider all the ways he deserves your praise in this moment, and then lift your hands as you pray out loud to him. Thank God for his goodness in your life and for allowing you to praise him in this way.

Apply

Make a note of the moments that make you want to lift your hands in praise this week. This could be a moment in which you achieve a special victory, or a moment when you cheer on a friend or family member, or a moment when you finish a big project at work, or even a moment when you hear a certain song on the radio. Whatever it is that causes you to raise your hands wherever you are, take a minute to stop and write it down.

DAY TWO: *YADAH* THROUGH THE EYES OF KING DAVID

Seek

■ Read Psalm 145. In this psalm, King David highlights two expressions of praise *shabach* (see verse 4) and *yadah* (see verse 10). How is lifting your hands in *yadah* praise different than giving a *shabach* shout of praise? What motivates you to lift your hands instead of shout in praise?

■ Look at verses 10–13. What does *yadah* praise "tell" about God in this passage?

■ Based on what you know about King David's life, what reasons did he have to praise God with his arms lifted high?

■ Raising your hands in praise says something not only about you but also about the One to whom you are raising your hands. What does your life "tell" about God? If your friends and family were to describe God based on his reflection in your life, what would they say?

■ If you could put words to the action of raising your hands in praise, what would those words be? Write down whatever comes to mind (for example, names of God, words of praise, fruits of the spirit, or words of celebration).

Reflect

■ Listen to or re-read the lyrics of "Holy Is the Lord." What especially stands out to you in this song, now that you've heard it or read the lyrics more than once?

■ How do you see the earth being "full of [God's] glory"? What is the evidence in this day and age that God is still at work and present in your everyday life?

Take time to pray today. Ask God to give you eyes to see his holiness and his glory all around you—and then give him praise for it. Contemplate the fact that *you* are an image-bearer of God in all his glory. And, as a member of a community of fellow image-bearers, together, you have the opportunity to shine with the holiness and glory of God.

Apply

Every time you express *yadah* praise to God this week, consider the word, thought, or emotion that causes you to raise your hands in worship. Is it God's love, his forgiveness, his glory, his grace in your life? Whatever it is, say it out loud so that every time your hands shoot out or up in praise, you whisper the reason why. This is one way to develop a new pattern of participating in the posture of praise.

DAY THREE: *BARAK* IN THE NEW TESTAMENT

Seek

■ Read Romans 14 (take special note of verse 11) and Acts 20:32–38. Notice how *barak* praise is often accompanied by a spirit of gratitude and thanksgiving . . . even in the midst of disagreement and grief. What stands out to you about the form of praise that Paul describes in Romans 14? What else in this passage stands out to you?

■ What stands out to you about the posture of worship depicted in Acts 20:32–38? What else stands out to you in this passage?

■ In your own words, how would you define *barak* praise?

■ How do you personally participate in this kind of praise?

■ Where and when do you see the most common occurrences of *barak* praise in our culture?

■ Read Revelation 4:10–11. Why do the elders fall down in worship before the throne of God?

Reflect

■ Read Philippians 2:5–11. How does Paul say Jesus' humility led to him being "exalted . . . to the highest place" (verse 9)?

■ What are you saying about Jesus and his place in your life when you kneel before him?

Take time to pray today. Put *barak* praise into action by kneeling and looking up to God. If this is not physically possible for you, then sit in whatever posture works best as a posture of praise. Just lift your eyes up to God and imagine looking into his eyes as you give him your praise. Tell him the place that he has in your life, and ask for him to continue to lead and guide you.

Apply

Try kneeling to pray several times today and notice how this posture changes your prayer life. Be sure to say a short sentence of praise every time you catch yourself kneeling in everyday life—to find your shoes under your bed, get your phone when it slides under your car seat, or when you tie your shoes. Use everyday moments of kneeling to offer *barak* praise to God.

DAY FOUR: *YADAH* AND *BARAK* IN A SEASON OF PAIN

Seek

■ Read Lamentations 3:1–41. Notice the range of emotions the prophet Jeremiah expresses in these verses! What are a few of the emotions you hear these "laments" of Jeremiah?

■ Even in the midst of this pain, Jeremiah recognizes he can praise God "because of the Lord's great love" and be thankful that his compassions "are new every morning" (verses 22–23). What does this tell you that Jeremiah had learned about God?

■ Why does Jeremiah encourage his audience (the people of Judah) to lift up their hearts and their hands to God in heaven (verse 41), even in the midst of their pain?

■ What is causing you pain today? What are some reasons you can name for why you can still praise God even in the midst of that pain?

Reflect

■ In the ancient world, *barak* involved kneeling before a person in authority and also maintaining eye contact with that individual. To refuse to kneel before the person meant that you did not respect him or her . . . which could lead to serious consequences. Read Esther 3:1–6. Who was the person of honor in this passage? Who showed respect to this individual?

■ Why didn't Mordecai kneel to this person? What were the consequences of his inaction?

Take time to pray today. Thank God today that he is worthy of all your praise and honor. Name some of the blessings that he has given to you—even if you are in the midst of difficult circumstances. Seek to keep your gaze focused on him as you go through your day.

Apply

Search your heart today and ask God if there is any area of your life that you haven't completely surrendered to him. Take a few minutes to submit anything he reveals to you to his authority. Ask God to help you focus on the example of Christ and practice humility. Acknowledge that he is the Lord of your life and commit to obeying his commands.

DAY FIVE: A POSTURE OF PRAISE

Seek

■ Read Psalm 103. This psalm begins (verses 1–2) and ends (verses 20–22) with *barak* praise, but if you didn't know the Hebrew words, you might think the author is referring to *yadah* praise. The difference is in the *posture* of praise. How does this change your perspective on the way David and the heavenly hosts praise the Lord? How would the text seem different to you if David was referring to *yadah* praise?

■ While vulnerability and surrender are key elements of *yadah* praise, gratitude and thanksgiving and reverence seem to be key elements of *barak* praise. How have you heard or seen these elements expressed in *barak* praise?

■ Now that you've had a few days to explore these postures of praise, what is it that most brings you to your knees in a posture of praise? What is it that causes you to lift your hands in a posture of praise?

■ Consider your surroundings. Where do you feel the most freedom to lift your hands in praise? Where do you experience the most freedom to fall on your knees in praise?

Reflect

■ Listen to or read the lyrics of the song "We Fall Down" by Chris Tomlin. What stands out to you in this song now that you understand the idea of *yadah* and *barak* praise?

■ What does it look like, or mean, for you to "lay" your own "crowns down" at the feet of Jesus every day? What are some of those crowns—the things or relationships or identities that make you feel special or seem significant?

Take time to pray today. Kneel down, if possible, and imagine taking off your "crowns" one by one as you pray. Let your prayer go something like this: "God, I give you this crown . . ." and then name whatever it is that crown represents—the person or thing that gives you significance and feeds your identity. Then move on to the next "crown." When you are done naming your crowns, lift your hands in praise for God's goodness and presence in your life.

Apply

Find a few pictures that remind you of the "crowns" in your life. Post those pictures in a place where you will see them throughout the day—in your closet, in your office, on your computer screen, on your pantry door, or in your locker at school. Be mindful to offer a prayer of gratitude and surrender every time you see those pictures as your praise to God.

FOR NEXT WEEK

Use the space below to write down any key points or questions that you want to bring to the next group meeting. In preparation for next week, read chapters 3 and 6 in *Holy Roar*.

three

THE MUSIC OF PRAISE

Praise is the rehearsal of our eternal song. By grace we learn to sing and in glory we continue to sing. What will some of you do when you get to heaven if you go on grumbling all the way? Do not hope to get to heaven in that style! But now, begin to bless the name of the Lord!

Charles Haddon Spurgeon,
The Keynote of the Year
(January 5, 1890)

תְּהִלָּה

TEHILLAH

teh-hil-law': Laudation. A hymn. A song of praise. A new song. A spontaneous song.

But You are holy, enthroned in the praises [tehillah] of Israel.

Psalm 22:3 NKJV

זָמַר

ZAMAR

zaw-mar': To make music. To celebrate in song and music. To touch the strings or parts of musical instruments.

I will sing a new song to You, O God; on a harp of ten strings I will sing praises [zamar] to You.

Psalm 144:9 NKJV

WELCOME

Do you ever catch yourself singing a random tune about your day? You find something funny, so you make up a little song about it. You get frustrated at work, so you let out a little stress by singing about it. You feel embarrassed by something you did or said, so you belt out a few spontaneous lyrics and then go straight into the chorus of "Let It Go" from the Disney movie.

All of this may sound like just comic relief, but the reality is that many researchers believe we were *wired* to create spontaneous songs like this. In fact, scientists believe the ability to sing and the ability to speak are directly related . . . and there is an increasing amount of research to support the idea that music has biological roots. So, whether you realize it or not, every time you sing a spontaneous song, you're actually warming up for the Hebrew word *tehillah*— offering a spontaneous song of praise to God. These are the simple songs of praise you sing or hum to God wherever you go—in your car, in the shower, inside your head at work, or while you're in the middle of the everyday mundane with your kids.

There's also something about singing (or even listening to music) that just seems to ease our minds and relax our bodies. The movie *The King's Speech* tells the story of a man, known to his family as "Bertie," who makes an improbable rise to the English throne when his brother abdicates. The problem is that Bertie has a speech impediment . . . which is an issue because English royals have to deliver public addresses. Bertie and his wife, Elizabeth, visit many different speech therapists, who try all kinds of strange therapies to cure him, but to no avail.

Frustrated, Bertie gives up. But Elizabeth convinces him to see one more therapist—a man named Lionel Logue. During one session, Lionel records the king reading lines out loud from *Hamlet* while listening to music blaring over headphones. To the king's surprise, when he later listens to the recording, he finds his stammer is completely gone. There is something about how the music occupies the king's mind that allows him to speak flawlessly.

Perhaps this is the same reason why Old Testament prophets like Elisha and ancient kings like Saul requested a harp player during moments of difficult decision-making or when they were anxious. The Hebrew word that captures this kind of instrumental underscoring to praise is *zamar*. Today, we'll look more closely at each of these Hebrew words for *praise*.

SHARE

Welcome to the third session of *Holy Roar*. Begin your group time by taking a few minutes to share any insights you wrote down from last week's personal study. Then, to kick things off, discuss one of the following questions:

- Do you remember a time when you made up your own spontaneous song about something? Are you willing to share that song with the group?

—or—

- Are there certain things you do better, faster, or easier while listening to music in the background? How do you find the music helps you?

WATCH

Play the video segment for session three. As you watch, use the following outline to record any thoughts or concepts that stand out to you.

Notes

Tehillah is the Hebrew word for _____. It is translated _____,
_____, or _____. But it is a little more than that, for *tehillah*
refers to . . .

Singing a new song about our particular story . . .

> *But You are holy, enthroned in the praises*
> [tehillah] *of Israel* (Psalm 22:3 NKJV).

When we choose to sing a spontaneous song out of the overflow of
gratitude in our lives . . .

> *Sing to the LORD a new song; sing to the*
> *LORD, all the earth* (Psalm 96:1).

Zamar is also translated as the English word _____, and it means
to _____ or part of _____.
The impact *zamar* has on the human soul . . .

> *I will sing a new song to You, O God; on*
> *a harp of ten strings I will sing praises*
> *[zamar] to You* (Psalm 144:9 NKJV).

What is required to participate in *zamar* . . .

Why "Good Good Father" is a perfect song for the word *tehillah* . . .

God can use each of our individual stories as we . . .

GROUP DISCUSSION

Take a few minutes with your group members to discuss what you just watched and explore these concepts in Scripture.

1. What are a few key points that stood out to you from this session?

2. Think about the story Darren told of singing spontaneous songs of gratitude for his family. What causes you to sing spontaneous songs of prayer and praise to God?

3. Think of what Chris shared regarding the back story of the song "Good Good Father." Has there been a time when you found yourself praying for a request that seemed beyond miraculous, or when you found yourself singing words of praise in the middle of immense pain for yourself or for others? Share briefly about that time.

4. Read aloud Psalm 96. What do you think the psalmist means by singing a "new" song to the Lord? What else stands out to you in this passage regarding praise?

5. Read aloud Psalm 57. This is a song David wrote as he fled from King Saul. What difference does music make for David during this time? Considering this example, how has music made a difference in your life?

6. What might keep you from putting these two words of praise, *tehillah* and *zamar,* into practice—either individually or corporately? Explain.

RESPOND

Close out today's session by briefly reviewing the outline for the video teaching and any notes you took. In the space below, write down the most significant point you took away from the session and why it is meaningful for you. If there's time, share your answer with the group.

WORSHIP

Consider worshiping together as you close out your group discussion. Play "Good Good Father" on your streaming device, or ask someone in your group if they would be willing to play it on a musical instrument. As you listen, think about the story Chris shared during the teaching of how the song came to be written, and consider what spontaneous words of praise you want to say to God in this moment. Close by spending a few minutes in prayer together.

Good Good Father

I've heard a thousand stories of what they think you're like
But I've heard the tender whispers of love in the dead of night
And you tell me that you're pleased
And that I'm never alone

You're a good good father
It's who you are, it's who you are, it's who you are
And I'm loved by you
It's who I am, it's who I am, it's who I am

I've seen many searching for answers far and wide
But I know we're all searching
For answers only you provide
'Cause you know just what we need
Before we say a word

You're a good good father
It's who you are, it's who you are, it's who you are
And I'm loved by you
It's who I am, it's who I am, it's who I am

Because you are perfect in all of your ways
You are perfect in all of your ways
You are perfect in all of your ways to us

You are perfect in all of your ways
You are perfect in all of your ways
You are perfect in all of your ways to us

Oh, it's love so undeniable
I, I can hardly speak
Peace so unexplainable
I, I can hardly think
As you call me deeper still
As you call me deeper still
As you call me deeper still
Into love, love, love

You're a good good father
It's who you are, it's who you are, it's who you are
And I'm loved by you
It's who I am, it's who I am, it's who I am

You're a good good father
It's who you are, it's who you are, it's who you are
And I'm loved by you
It's who I am, it's who I am, it's who I am
You're a good good father

It's who you are, it's who you are, it's who you are
And I'm loved by you
It's who I am, it's who I am, it's who I am
You're a good good father

You are perfect in all of your ways
It's who you are, it's who you are, it's who you are
And I'm loved by you
You are perfect in all of your ways
It's who I am, it's who I am, it's who I am

Songwriters: Pat Barrett and Anthony Brown.
Performed by Chris Tomlin on the album *Never Lose Sight*.

three

BETWEEN-SESSIONS PERSONAL STUDY

Reflect on the content you've covered this week in *Holy Roar* by engaging in any or all of the following between-sessions activities. The time you invest will be well spent, so let God use it to draw you closer to him. At your next meeting, share with your group any key points or insights that stood out to you as you spent this time with the Lord.

DAY ONE: SINGING A NEW SONG OF *TEHILLAH*

Seek

■ Read the following passages from the Bible: Psalm 33:3; 96:1; 98:1; 144:9; 149:1; and Isaiah 42:10–13. *Tehillah* wasn't just a passive idea used to encourage the Israelites to sing. Why do you think this phrase appears so often throughout the psalms?

■ Why do you think the Israelites were given a command to sing a "new" song instead of a familiar song of praise?

■ Pause and try singing a new song to God in this moment. How is this experience different for you than singing a familiar song or praying a familiar prayer?

■ When would be the best time for you to practice *tehillah*? Would it be in the car on your way to work, or when working in your yard, or during your morning run, or while playing with your kids? Think about this and write down a time you could practice *tehillah*.

Reflect

■ Reflect on the story Chris shared about the song "Good Good Father" and how he played it for his girls at bedtime. Was there a song or anthem you used to sing at bedtime as a child . . . or perhaps a song your parents or caregiver sang to you? What was that experience like for you?

■ What does it mean for God to be a good, good Father?

Take time to pray today. The song "Good Good Father" was actually written by a man who never knew his own biological father. If this is your situation as well, ask God to show you what it means for him to be a good, good father in your life. Thank him for the way he loves you, for the way he provides for you, and for his constant presence in your life.

Apply

Add *tehillah* to your daily rhythm of spending time with God. Practice expressing your praise to God in spontaneous song in whatever place you identified as being the most comfortable for you. Consider how this spontaneous act of praise can change your relationship with God, and make note of any changes as you experience them.

DAY TWO: *TEHILLAH* THROUGH THE EYES OF KING DAVID

Seek

■ Read Psalm 40. God put a new song in David's heart in the midst of a difficult trial. What are the reasons David lists for singing a new song to God? How did God help David?

■ What are the attributes of God that David lists in this psalm that make him worthy of praise?

■ What are the reasons in your own life for singing a new song to God? How has God helped you?

■ What attributes of God have you experienced the most in your life? His mercy, grace, patience, forgiveness, deliverance, love, provision? Explain.

■ God didn't just give David a new song in his heart but he also placed David's "feet on a rock" and provided him "a firm place to stand" (verse 2). How has God placed your feet on a rock or given you a firm place to stand?

Reflect

■ Listen to or re-read the lyrics of "Good Good Father." What stands out to you in this song, now that you've heard it more than once?

■ How has God guided you recently like a good, good father?

Take time to pray today. Thank God for his promise that "his love endures forever" (Psalm 136). Reflect on how God has been a good father *through* your own earthly father or *in spite of* your own earthly father. Consider the ways he has shown his love for you and his faithfulness to you, and ask him to heal any "father wounds" you carry with you.

Apply

Create your own song of *tehillah* to God today. Don't overthink it. Just let your words of love and gratitude flow freely from your heart and mind to your mouth. It's okay to be silly in your spontaneous song if that gives you freedom in the moment. God delights in your joy as well!

DAY THREE: *ZAMAR* IN THE OLD TESTAMENT

Seek

■ Read the story of Elisha in 2 Kings 3:1–20, and the story of Saul and David in 1 Samuel 16:14–23. What stands out to you about *zamar* praise in the story of Elisha? What happens as a result of *zamar*?

■ What stands out to you about *zamar* praise in the story of David and King Saul? What happens as a result of *zamar*?

■ How does your faith community participate in *zamar* praise? How and where does *zamar* show up in our culture?

■ How have you specifically practiced *zamar* praise? What kind of impact does music have in your everyday life? Does it calm you, help you concentrate, pump you up, or give you more creative freedom? Explain.

■ What kind of instrumental music has the greatest effect on you? Why?

Reflect

■ Listen to your favorite style of instrumental music for a few minutes. How do you feel after listening to that track? What did you think about or experience during that time?

■ Where is the most convenient time and place for you to practice *zamar* praise outside of your corporate church worship service?

Take time to pray today. Put *zamar* praise into action by again playing music as you pray. Notice what effect it has on you to "underscore" your prayer time with music. (If you find it is distracting to have the music playing, just allow yourself to settle by first listening or humming along, and then go into prayer once you're no longer feeling distracted.)

Apply

Devote another specific time today to pause and listen to instrumental music. Make this convenient for your schedule—such as when you're driving in the car on your way to and from work, while taking the dog out for an evening walk, over your lunch break, while you're working on a big project, while your kids are napping, and so on.

DAY FOUR: *ZAMAR* IN A SEASON OF TRIAL

Seek

■ Read Psalm 137:1–6. The words of this psalm reflect the anguish the Israelites felt after their nation was conquered by foreign invaders and they were led into captivity. What stands out to you in these verses? Why did the harpists hang up their harps?

■ Imagine a world without music. What would that be like from your perspective?

■ How has music lifted your spirits during a hard season? Is there a song or style of music that you feel speaks directly to you in those difficult times?

■ What songs tend to bring you comfort, healing, and hope during times of trial?

■ Read Revelation 14:2–3. What words would you use to describe the moment of instrumental music mentioned in this passage?

Reflect

■ Listen to your preferred style of instrumental music or try a new style for a few minutes. What stands out to you about the music now that you understand the idea of *zamar* praise?

■ What words would you use to describe the way music makes you feel, or the way music moves you, especially during a season of pain?

Take time to pray today. Share your past or present trials with God and ask him to remind you of the joy that is possible even in the midst of a difficult season. Pray for God to bring you a new song that speaks to your heart, mind, and soul. Also, be sure to thank God for the gift of music.

Apply

Name a specific pain or trial you are experiencing and assign a song to it. Listen to that song as you pray for the specific circumstances surrounding your trial. Do this as many times as needed to express what you are feeling to God and ask for his perfect peace in the situation.

DAY FIVE: *ZAMAR* AND *TEHILLAH* IN THE NEW TESTAMENT

Seek

■ Read Ephesians 5:8–20. In this passage, the apostle Paul talks about how the believers should sing spontaneous songs to each other and to God (*tehillah*) and make music from their heart to the Lord (*zamar*). Why do you think Paul gave this instruction to the Ephesians?

■ What else stands out to you in these verses?

■ Read Colossians 3:1–17. What similarities do you see in this passage when you compare it to Paul's words in Ephesians 5:8–20?

■ What else stands out to you in these verses?

■ Consider a modern-day approach to *tehillah* and *zamar*. How could believers in Christ incorporate this type of praise into their everyday lives in a way that expresses their joy, love, and gratitude toward God?

Reflect

■ Listen to or re-read the lyrics of "Good Good Father" one more time. How could you encourage a friend with this song? Who in your life needs to be reminded that God is a good father?

■ What is it like to experience a powerful worship set or instrumental music with a friend or a community of friends? Is this comfortable or uncomfortable for you? Why?

Take time to pray today. Ask God to show you how to incorporate more space for *tehillah* and *zamar* in your own life and in the life of your community. Thank God for the way he has used music to speak to your heart, mind, and soul. Ask God to show you how to love and encourage your community with music and spontaneous song in a way that is culturally relevant.

Apply

Consider a night of worship with your small group as part of your discussion experience or as a gathering set apart just for worship. Start your evening with a few of the songs mentioned in this study as you ease into times of instrumental praise and spontaneous songs of praise. The more you practice this style of praise, the more comfortable you will become with it.

FOR NEXT WEEK

Use the space below to write down any key points or questions that you want to bring to the next group meeting. In preparation for next week, read chapter 4 and the conclusion in *Holy Roar*.

four

THE EXPECTATION OF PRAISE

If the devil has a sense of humor, I think he must laugh and hold his sooty sides when he sees a church of dead Christians singing a hymn written by a spiritually awakened and worshipping composer. . . . True worship that is pleasing to God creates within the human heart a spirit of expectation and insatiable longing.

A.W. Tozer,
The Purpose of Man

תּוֹדָה

TOWDAH

to-daw': An extension of the hand.
Thanksgiving. A confession. A sacrifice
of praise. Thanksgiving for things not
yet received. A choir of worshippers.

*In God I have put my trust; I will not
be afraid. What can man do to me?
Vows made to You are binding upon me,
O God; I will render praises* [towdah] *to You.*

Psalm 56:11–12 NKJV

WELCOME

Do you remember what it was like as a kid when you realized the month of your birthday had arrived and the big day was only a few weeks away? Perhaps this realization came about when you saw the date circled on the calendar on the fridge, or you noticed your mom had bought some birthday invitations to send to your friends, or you overheard your parents talking about what they would be doing for your party. These signs likely filled you with expectation of the presents, celebration, and overall joy that would soon be coming your way.

It was easy for you to be thankful when you saw these positive signs of good things to come. But it was likely more difficult to be thankful when such signs were not present—when your sports team was on a losing streak, or you were struggling in a class at school, or you were dealing with a bully, or you were having a conflict with a close friend. In these times of difficulty, it was hard for you to see the light at the end of the tunnel.

The apostle Paul certainly knew his share of difficult times. In his second letter to the believers in Corinth, he provides a list of some of the things he had endured as he spread the message of Christ—including beatings, shipwrecks, hunger, and dangers from all sides. Scholars believe that by the time he wrote his letter to the Philippians, he was likely in chains in a prison in the city of Rome. Yet in spite of his troubles, he could still write, "Do not be anxious about anything, but in every situation, by prayer and petition, with thanksgiving, present your requests to God. And the peace of God, which transcends all understanding, will guard your hearts and your minds in Christ Jesus" (Philippians 4:6–7).

Paul had learned the secret of what the Hebrew psalmists referred to as *towdah*. This refers to lifting your hands as a "sacrifice of praise" (Hebrews 13:15) . . . to thank God not only for what you have received so far but also for what you have *not* yet received. *Towdah* is an attitude of praise and worship toward God even when the signs of something good to come are not present. This type of praise requires a steadfast belief that "in all things God works for the good of those who love him, who have been called according to his purpose" (Romans 8:28).

As you might imagine, this is the most challenging of all the expressions of praise that we have discussed during this study. But it is also one of the most important aspects of worship for us to grasp. Today, we will look more closely at this particular type of praise.

SHARE

Welcome to the final session of *Holy Roar.* Begin your group time by taking a few minutes to share any insights you wrote down from last week's personal study. Then, to get things started, discuss one of the following questions:

- Has there ever been a time when you were so discouraged you didn't think you could praise or worship God? What did you do in that situation?

—*or*—

- How has a particular worship song or worship experience ministered to you during a difficult season in your life?

WATCH

Play the video segment for session four. As you watch, use the following outline to record any thoughts or concepts that stand out to you.

Notes

The Hebrew word *towdah* means to lift your hands as _____
_____. It means to thank God for what you
_____ and _____ _____ received from him.

> *Some trust in chariots and some in*
>
> *horses, but we trust in the name of*
>
> *the LORD our God* (Psalm 20:7).

When we are praising God, what we are declaring is . . .

> *In God I have put my trust; I will not be*
>
> *afraid. . . . I will render praises* [towdah]
>
> *to You* (Psalm 56:11–12 NKJV).

As Christians, we need to be reminding one another of . . .

[Speak] to one another with psalms, hymns, and songs from the Spirit. Sing and make music from your heart to the Lord (Ephesians 5:19).

Towdah is such a different Hebrew word for praise than the others because . . .

The power of praise in the midst of anxiety and sleepless nights . . .

What enables us to praise God in the midst of any storm . . .

The one place at least in which all believers should be together in unity . . .

The seven Hebrew words of praise don't just tell us *who* to praise but also . . .

Praise the L*ORD*. *Praise God in his sanctuary;
praise him in his mighty heavens. Praise him for
his acts of power; praise him for his surpassing
greatness. Praise him with the sounding of the
trumpet, praise him with the harp and lyre, praise
him with tambourine and dancing, praise him with
the strings and flute, praise him with the clash of
cymbals, praise him with resounding cymbals.
Let everything that has breath praise the* L*ORD*.
Praise the L*ORD* (Psalm 150:1–6 NIV 1984).

DISCUSS

Take a few minutes with your group members to discuss what you
just watched and explore these concepts in Scripture.

1. What are a few key points that stood out to you from this session?

2. Think about the story Darren told of speaking at the largest
   African American church in Chicagoland. When is a time you
   have been inspired by the faith of others in spite of the difficulties going on in their lives? Explain.

3. Consider what Chris shared in regard to writing the lyrics for "I Lift My Hands." When is a time you have walked alongside a friend who was hurting and in need? What are some songs of praise that helped you and your friend through that time?

4. Read aloud Psalm 42. What is the longing you hear in this psalm of *towdah* praise? How can you identify with the thoughts expressed by the psalmist?

5. Read aloud Psalm 56. King David wrote this psalm when he was seized by the Philistines in Gath (see 1 Samuel 21:10–15). What are some of the troubles that David names in this psalm? How does he resolve to thank God in spite of those difficulties?

6. How does your church celebrate *towdah*? How can you better celebrate *towdah* with your fellow brothers and sisters in Christ?

RESPOND

Close out today's session by briefly reviewing the outline for the video teaching and any notes you took. In the space below, write down the most significant point you took away from the session and why it is meaningful for you. If there's time, share your answer with the group.

WORSHIP

Consider worshiping together as you close out this study. Play "I Lift My Hands" on your streaming device, or ask someone in your group if they would be willing to play it on a musical instrument. Focus on the words of the song and think about the ways in which they capture the essence of *towdah*. Close by spending a few minutes in prayer together.

I Lift My Hands

Be still, there is a healer
His love is deeper than the sea
His mercy, it is unfailing
His arms are a fortress for the weak

Let faith arise
Let faith arise

I lift my hands to believe again
You are my refuge, You are my strength
As I pour out my heart, these things I remember
You are faithful, God, forever

Be still, there is a river
That flows from Calvary's tree
A fountain for the thirsty
Pure grace that washes over me

So let faith arise
Let faith arise
Open my eyes
Open my eyes

I lift my hands to believe again
You are my refuge, You are my strength
As I pour out my heart, these things I remember
You are faithful, God
You are faithful, God, forever

Songwriters: Chris Tomlin, Louie Giglio, and Matt Maher.
From the album *And If Our God Is for Us . . .*

four

FINAL PERSONAL STUDY

Reflect on the content you've covered during this final week in *Holy Roar* by engaging in any or all of the following activities. The time you invest will be well spent, so let God use it to draw you closer to him. Be sure to share with your group leader or group members in the upcoming weeks any key points or insights that stood out to you.

DAY ONE: *TOWDAH* ENCOURAGEMENT FOR THE ISRAELITES

Seek

■ Read Psalm 20. King David wrote this psalm as an encouragement to his fellow Israelites. He was reminding them (and us) that when God's people raise their hands high in praise, they are pointing to their ultimate source of hope. According to David, how does God respond to you when you are in distress?

■ How has God given you the "desire of your heart" and made "all your plans succeed" (verse 4)?

■ How have you shouted "for joy" or lifted up your "banners in the name of our God" in response to God's protection and provision in your life (verse 5)?

■ David writes, "Some trust in chariots and some in horses, but we trust in the name of the LORD our God" (verse 7). What are a few modern-day examples of where people place their trust?

■ In what specific areas of life do you need God to "answer . . . when [you] call" (verse 9)? How do you specifically need him to help you "rise up and stand firm" (verse 8)?

Reflect

■ Think about the story Chris shared in writing the song "I Lift My Hands." The song actually comes from the story of his friend Louie Giglio, who would wake up in the night and sing a little phrase during those times when anxiety kept him awake. Can you relate to Louie's experience? What tends to run through your mind when you can't sleep?

■ Is there a verse or poem, song or phrase that has carried you through your own difficult season of restless nights?

Take time to pray today. There's a good chance someone in your life is wrestling through a difficult season today. Ask God to make his presence known to whomever may be struggling around you. Pray for God to bring comfort, love, and healing during this difficult season. And ask him to show you who is struggling—who needs an encouraging word, a kind deed, or a thoughtful prayer—so you can be a loving reflection of God to the world around you.

Apply

If certain individuals came to mind during your prayer time today, reach out to them and let them know you are here for them. If you sense a need, follow through on meeting it. Remember this doesn't have to be all on you . . . you can enlist the help of your small group or local community to meet those needs. And if *you* are the one struggling today, reach out and share your struggles with a friend. This may be what you need to rise up and stand firm today!

DAY TWO: *TOWDAH* THROUGH THE EYES OF KING DAVID

Seek

■ Re-read Psalm 56. In verse 3, King David says, "When I am afraid, I put my trust in you." Why was King David so afraid here?

■ Where do you place your trust when you are feeling afraid? In your spouse or significant other, in your boss, in your parents, your teacher, in yourself, or in God? Explain.

■ How has God answered your cry for help in the past? How has God responded to your *towdah* praise—when you have praised him with expectation of what he will do in your life?

■ David says, "In God, whose word I praise, in the Lord, whose word I praise . . ." (verse 10). David did not yet have the Word (the Bible) as we know it today. What, then, do you think he means when he refers to "God's word" in this passage?

■ How has God kept you from stumbling? How has God rescued you from a difficult time?

Reflect

■ Listen to or re-read the lyrics of I "Lift My Hands." What stands out to you in this song?

■ One of the lyrics in the song is "let faith arise." What does it look like to let faith arise in you when you are feeling low? How have you witnessed or contributed to faith arising in the life of someone around you?

Take time to pray today. Pray through the descriptions of God in this song. Thank God for being a healer and that his love is deeper than the sea. Thank the Lord for his unfailing mercy and his arms that surround you like a fortress. Ask God to allow your faith to arise in this season.

Apply

Journal about what it looks like for your faith to arise. Is it spending time in prayer and reading the Bible at the beginning or end of your day? Is it making a gratitude list of everything for which you are thankful? Is it making a commitment to be positive in your work environment? Is it seeking help for anxiety and depression? Describe what it looks like for your faith to arise using these action statements or phrases, and then commit to doing at least one today.

DAY THREE: *TOWDAH* IN THE NEW TESTAMENT

Seek

■ Read Hebrews 11. This chapter in the Bible is commonly referred to as the "Faith Hall of Fame." All of the individuals listed in this passage lived by faith . . . trusting that God was who he said he was and would do what he said he would do. What stands out to you in these verses?

■ Is there a particular person you relate to the most? If so, why?

■ How does the author define faith in verse 1?

■ Biblical scholars believe the author of Hebrews was writing to a group of people from a Jewish background who were suffering some form of persecution for their faith. Given this, why did the author choose to include this reminder of the "ancients" and their faith?

■ Who are the people who have inspired you with their *towdah* praise and their faith? How have they specifically inspired you?

Reflect

■ Re-read or listen to "I Lift My Hands." When you offer *towdah* praise, it is because you are expecting God to be faithful—and you are declaring your trust in him *even before* he has answered your prayers. Have you raised your hands in praise, believing in faith that God will fulfill his promises to you? If not, what is holding you back?

■ In what area do you need to offer *towdah* praise today, believing that God will come through for you?

Take time to pray today. There is something powerful that happens when God's people speak their requests to God out loud. Perhaps you've been praying silent prayers so far during this study, but today your encouragement is to *pray out loud*. Practice *towdah* by stretching out your hands, palms up, and speaking your prayer requests to God. At the end of your prayer, give thanks to God for the things he *has done* and *will do* in your life.

Apply

Write out your requests to God on a piece of paper or post-it note and place it where you will see it on a regular basis. Every time you look at that list, offer a brief moment of *towdah* praise to God for what you are believing he will do. Or you can make this list for the requests of your friends. Explain *towdah* praise to them and let them know you are believing God's faithfulness *with* them and *for* them.

DAY FOUR: THE RHYTHMS OF PRAISE

Seek

■ Read Psalm 134 and Psalm 119:164–165. In spite of their differences, the people of Israel made a pilgrimage three times a year to worship in the temple in Jerusalem. On their way to the temple, they sang the same songs each year, known as the "psalms of ascents." These songs were significant because they culminated in a unifying declaration of praise before God as their king. The Israelites also paused for praise on a regular basis throughout their daily lives. Both of these rhythms were individual and collective. What else stands out to you in these verses?

■ What can you learn from the way the Israelites practiced these rhythms of praise on a consistent basis—yearly, weekly, and daily?

■ Consider your own life. In what rhythms of praise do you participate on your own? Your personal prayer time, weekend worship at church, a concert with friends, a special night of worship with your small group community? Explain.

■ From your perspective, what effect does it have on believers in Christ to have consistent praise both in community and as individuals?

Reflect

■ Listen to or read the lyrics of your favorite worship song. (If you don't have a particular favorite, pick a song mentioned in this study or in the *Holy Roar* book.) What kind of praise is being offered in that song?

■ How does the song speak to you or minister to you in this particular season of life?

Take time to pray today. Thank God for the role worship and praise have played in your relationship with him. Thank him for the opportunity you have to praise him each and every day, even during the challenging seasons of life. And if you're in one of those seasons now, ask God to give you the desire to worship and the words to praise his name.

Apply

The goal today is to incorporate a more consistent rhythm of praise into your life. Are there moments throughout your day when you could pause to listen to a song and spend a few minutes in worship? If so, assign a song for each one of those moments. You could have a song for the morning, for your drive to work, for listening to over lunch, for making dinner, and a song at the end of the day as you climb into bed. If this seems a bit overwhelming, pick a worship song for the week and listen to it a few times a day. The idea is not to find the *perfect* song for the right time but to find a consistent *rhythm* of praise in your everyday life.

DAY FIVE: THE SEVEN WORDS OF PRAISE

Seek

■ Read Psalm 122. Unity is found when we praise the Lord together, just as the Israelites were doing here in this psalm of ascent. When followers of Jesus gather together to praise, denominational divisions disappear as we lift our voices as *one* to God. This is why God's desire for a full expression of praise isn't contingent on our personalities or preferred styles of worship. And if you continue to explore the depths of these seven Hebrew words of praise and take them to heart, you too will find freedom in the full expression of praise. What in particular stands out to you in this psalm?

■ What do you think a full expression of praise looked like for these Israelites as they sang out their songs on the way to Jerusalem? How did they rejoice together? What was their unified prayer as they made their journey?

■ Consider the seven words of praise. In which areas of praise do you desire more freedom of expression? What can you do to better express those types of praise?

■ Which expressions of praise are most encouraged in your denomination or in your church family? Which expressions are the least encouraged?

■ What could a full expression of praise look like in your church community if everyone understood these seven words of praise?

Reflect

■ Go back and listen to the song "I Lift My Hands" one more time. Or, if there is another song that stood out to you from this study, listen to that song as you take time to reflect. How has your perspective of praise changed as a result of this study?

■ What will you *start* doing in times of worship and praise? What will you *stop* doing in times of worship and praise?

Take time to pray today. Remember that worship is meant to be a whole-being and everyday practice—a practice that God doesn't just *desire* but actually *requires*. So ask God to give you the wisdom and commitment to incorporate some form of worship in your everyday life. Pray about what this looks like for you as you consider your priorities, and pay attention to what you sense God is saying to you.

Apply

Share what you've learned about worship through this study with your small group leader or your worship leader. If it's not possible to sit down and share your story in person, then write a note or send that person an email to share the top two or three ways God has shaped or changed your perspective on worship as a result of this study. Keep in mind that it's more important for you to share what you've learned than it is for you to suggest changes to your weekly worship service. If you wish things would look different at your church, first make the necessary changes in your own rhythms of praise and worship, and then look for opportunities to participate in or encourage the worship culture of your church family.

Thank you for joining us for *Holy Roar!*

LEADER'S GUIDE

Thank you for your willingness to lead your group through this study! What you have chosen to do is valuable and will make a great difference in the lives of others. The rewards of being a leader are different from those of participating, and we hope that as you lead you will find your own walk with Jesus deepened by this experience.

Holy Roar is a four-session study built around video content and small-group interaction. As the group leader, just think of yourself as the host of a dinner party. Your job is to take care of your guests by managing all the behind-the-scenes details so that when everyone arrives, they can just enjoy time together.

As the group leader, your role is not to answer all the questions or reteach the content—the video, book, and study guide will do most of that work. Your job is to guide the experience and cultivate your small group into a kind of teaching community. This will make it a place for members to process, question, and reflect—not receive more instruction.

Before your first meeting, make sure everyone in the group gets a copy of the study guide. This will keep everyone on the same page and help the process run more smoothly. If some group members are unable to purchase the guide, arrange it so that people can share the resource with other group members. Giving everyone access to all the material will position this study to be as rewarding an experience as possible. Everyone should feel free to write in his or her study guide and bring it to the meeting every week.

SETTING UP THE GROUP

You will need to determine with your group how long you want to meet each week so you can plan your time accordingly. Generally, most groups like to meet for either sixty minutes or ninety minutes, so you could use one of the following schedules:

Section	60 minutes	90 minutes
WELCOME (members arrive and get settled)	5 minutes	10 minutes
SHARE (discuss one or more of the opening questions for the session)	5 minutes	10 minutes
VIDEO (watch the teaching material together and take notes)	20 minutes	20 minutes
DISCUSS (discuss the Bible study questions you selected ahead of time)	20 minutes	40 minutes
RESPOND & WORSHIP (note key takeaways, pray together, and dismiss)	10 minutes	10 minutes

As the group leader, you will want to create an environment that encourages sharing and learning. A church sanctuary or formal classroom may not be as ideal as a living room, because those locations can feel formal and less intimate. No matter what setting you choose, provide enough comfortable seating for everyone, and, if possible, arrange the seats in a semicircle so everyone can see the video easily. This will make the transition between the video and group conversation more efficient and natural.

Also, try to get to the meeting site early so you can greet participants as they arrive. Simple refreshments create a welcoming atmosphere and can be a wonderful addition to a group study evening. Try to take food and pet allergies into account to make your guests as comfortable as possible. You may also want to consider offering childcare to couples with children who want to attend. Finally, be sure your media technology is working properly. Managing these details up front will make the rest of your group experience flow smoothly and provide a welcoming space in which to engage the content of *Holy Roar*.

STARTING THE GROUP TIME

Once everyone has arrived, it's time to begin the group. Here are some simple tips to make your group time healthy, enjoyable, and effective.

First, begin the meeting with a short prayer and remind the group members to put their phones on silent. This is a way to make sure you can all be present with one another and with God. Next, give each person a few minutes to respond to the questions in the "Share" section. This won't require as much time in session one, but beginning in session two, people will need more time to share their insights from their personal studies. Usually, you won't answer the discussion questions yourself, but you should go first with the "Share" questions, answering briefly and with a reasonable amount of transparency.

At the end of session one, invite the group members to complete the between-sessions personal studies for that week. Explain that you will be providing some time before the video teaching next week for anyone to share insights. Let them know sharing is optional, and it's no problem if they can't get to some of the between-sessions activities some weeks. It will still be beneficial for them to hear from the other participants and learn about what they discovered.

LEADING THE DISCUSSION TIME

Now that the group is engaged, it is time to watch the video and respond with some directed small-group discussion. Encourage all the group members to participate in the discussion, but make sure they know they don't have to do so. As the discussion progresses, you may want to follow up with comments such as, "Tell me more about that . . . " or, "Why did you answer that way?" This will allow the group participants to deepen their reflections and invite meaningful sharing in a nonthreatening way.

Note that you have been given multiple questions to use in each session, and you do not have to use them all or even follow them in order. Feel free to pick and choose questions based on either the needs of your group or how the conversation is flowing. Also, don't be afraid of silence. Offering a question and allowing up to thirty seconds of silence is okay. It allows people space to think about how they want to respond and also gives them time to do so.

As group leader, you are the boundary keeper for your group. Do not let anyone (yourself included) dominate the group time. Keep an eye out for group members who might be tempted to "attack" folks they disagree with or try to "fix" those having struggles. These kinds of behaviors can derail a group's momentum, so they need to be steered in a different direction. Model active listening and encourage everyone in your group to do the same. This will make your group time a safe space and create a positive community.

The group discussion leads to a closing time of individual reflection and then worship as a group. Encourage the participants to review their key takeaways from the session and record their thoughts in the "Respond" section. This will help them cement the big ideas in their minds as you close the session.

Thank you again for taking the time to lead your group. You are making a difference in the lives of others and having an impact on the kingdom of God.

THE SEVEN HEBREW WORDS OF PRAISE IN THE PSALMS

T he following is a list of the psalms in the Bible that contain the seven Hebrew words for praise discussed in this study: *halal, shabach, yadah, barak, tehillah, zamar,* and *towdah.*

הָלַל halal

Psalm 5:5; 10:3; 18:3; 22:22, 23, 26; 34:2; 35:18; 44:8; 48:1; 49:6; 52:1; 56:4, 10 (two times); 63:5, 11; 64:10; 69:30, 34; 73:3; 74:21; 75:4 (two times); 78:63; 84:4; 96:4; 97:7; 102:8, 18; 104:35; 105:3, 45; 106:1, 5, 48; 107:32; 109:30; 111:1; 112:1; 113:1 (three times), 3, 9; 115:17, 18; 116:19; 117:1, 2; 119:164, 175; 135:1 (three times), 3, 21; 145:2–3, 145:3; 146:1 (two times), 2, 10; 147:1, 12, 20; 148:1 (three times), 2 (two times), 3 (two times), 4, 5, 7, 13, 14; 149:1, 3, 9; 150:1 (three times), 2 (two times), 3 (two times), 4 (two times), 5 (two times), 6 (two times).

שָׁבַח shabach

Psalm 63:3; 65:7; 89:9; 106:47; 117:1; 145:4; 147:12.

יָדָה yadah

Psalm 6:5; 7:17; 9:1; 18:49; 28:7; 30:4, 9, 12; 32:5; 33:2; 35:18; 42:5, 11; 43:4, 5; 44:8; 45:17; 49:18; 52:9; 54:6; 57:9; 67:3 (two times), 5 (two times); 71:22; 75:1 (two times); 76:10; 79:13; 86:12; 88:10; 89:5; 92:1; 97:12; 99:3; 100:4; 105:1; 106:1, 47; 107:1, 8, 15, 21, 31; 108:3; 109:30; 111:1; 118:1, 19, 21, 28, 29; 119:7, 62; 122:4; 136:1, 2, 3, 26; 138:1, 2, 4; 139:14; 140:13; 142:7; 145:10.

בָּרַךְ barak

Psalm 5:12; 10:3; 16:7; 18:46; 26:12; 28:6, 9; 29:11; 31:21; 34:1; 37:22; 41:13; 45:2; 49:18; 62:4; 63:4; 65:10; 66:8, 20; 67:1, 6, 7; 68:19, 26, 35; 72:15, 17, 18, 19; 89:52; 95:6; 96:2; 100:4; 103:1, 2, 20, 21, 22 (two times); 104:1, 35; 106:48; 107:38; 109:28; 112:2; 113:2; 115:12 (three times), 13, 15, 18; 118:26 (two times); 119:12; 124:6; 128:4, 5; 129:8; 132:15 (two times); 134:1, 2, 3; 135:19 (two times).

תְּהִלָּה tehillah

Psalm 9:14; 22:3, 25; 33:1; 34:1; 35:28; 40:3; 48:10; 51:15; 65:1; 66:2, 8; 71:6, 8, 14; 78:4; 79:13; 100:4; 102:21; 106:2, 12, 47; 109:1; 111:10; 119:171; 145:1, 21; 147:1; 148:14; 149:1.

זָמַר zamar

Psalm 7:17; 9:2, 11; 18:49, 50; 21:13; 27:6; 30:4, 12; 33:2; 47:6 (four times); 47:7; 57:7, 9; 59:17; 61:8; 66:2, 4 (two times); 68:4, 32; 71:22, 23; 75:9; 92:1; 98:4, 5; 101:1; 104:33; 105:2; 108:1, 3; 135:3; 138:1; 144:9; 146:2; 147:1, 7; 149:3.

תּוֹדָה towdah

Psalm 26:7; 42:4; 50:14, 23; 56:12; 69:30; 95:2; 100:1, 4; 107:22; 116:17; 147:7.

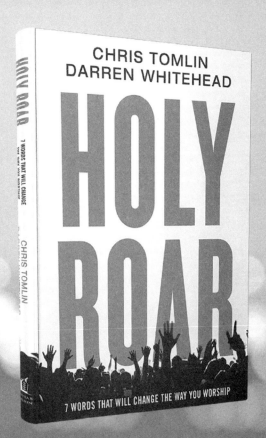